Better Homes and Gardens®

SUPER SNACKS

Our seal assures you that every recipe in *Super Snacks*
has been tested in the Better Homes and Gardens® Test Kitchen.
This means that each recipe is practical and reliable,
and meets our high standards of taste appeal.

For years, Better Homes and Gardens® Books has been a leader in publishing cook books. In *Super Snacks*, we've pulled together a delicious collection of recipes from several of our latest best-sellers. These no-fail recipes will make your cooking easier and more enjoyable.

Editor: Rosemary C. Hutchinson
Editorial Project Manager: Mary Helen Schiltz
Graphic Designer: Harijs Priekulis
Electronic Text Processor: Paula Forest

On the front cover: Meat and Melon Bites
(see recipe, page 13)

Contents

Snack Mix Ingredients

Tropical

- 1 cup cashews *or* macadamia nuts
- 1 cup coconut chips
- 1 tablespoon soy sauce
- ½ teaspoon garlic powder
- ½ teaspoon ground ginger

Barbecue

- 1 cup peanuts
- 1 tablespoon Worcester-shire sauce
- 1 teaspoon barbecue spice
  Dash garlic powder

Hot and Spicy

- 1 cup peanuts
- 2 teaspoons chili powder
- 1 teaspoon garlic powder
- 1 teaspoon bottled hot pepper sauce

Snack Mix Base

5 cups desired cereal
   (bite-size wheat squares
   cereal, bite-size rice
   squares cereal, bite-size
   corn squares cereal,
   round toasted oat
   cereal, bite-size
   shredded wheat
   biscuits, *or* crispy corn
   and rice cereal bites)
1½ cups chow mein noodles
   or pretzels
⅓ cup butter *or* margarine,
   melted
   Snack Mix Ingredients
   (see choices below)

● Combine desired cereal and chow mein noodles or pretzels in a 13x9x2-inch baking pan. Stir together melted butter or margarine and desired Snack Mix ingredients. Pour over cereal mixture, tossing gently till well coated. Bake in a 325°oven about 25 minutes, stirring once or twice. Spread in a large shallow pan or on foil to cool. Makes about 7½ cups.

Raid your cupboards— you're bound to come up with the makings for at least one of these six mixes.

Herbed Pecan

1 cup broken pecans
1 tablespoon dried parsley
   flakes
1 teaspoon dried thyme,
   crushed
½ teaspoon celery salt
½ teaspoon onion powder

Curry

1 cup peanuts
2 teaspoons curry powder
½ teaspoon crushed red
   pepper
¼ teaspoon onion salt

Traditional

1 cup mixed nuts
1 tablespoon Worcester-
   shire sauce
½ teaspoon seasoned salt
   Dash garlic powder

Pizzazz Mix

2½ cups oyster crackers
2½ cups bite-size shredded
     wheat biscuits
  1 cup round toasted oat
     cereal

● In an ungreased 15½x10½x2-inch baking pan combine oyster crackers, wheat biscuits, and oat cereal. Set cereal mixture aside.

If you like lots of pizzazz, shake on the hot pepper sauce with a heavy hand.

½ cup cooking oil
¼ teaspoon garlic salt
¼ teaspoon dried oregano,
     crushed
¼ teaspoon dried basil,
     crushed
  3 drops bottled hot pepper
     sauce

● In a small saucepan combine oil, garlic salt, oregano, basil, and hot pepper sauce. Heat over low heat for 2 minutes.

  2 tablespoons grated
     Parmesan cheese

● Stir oil mixture till well blended. Drizzle over cereal mixture and toss gently to coat cereal evenly.
    Bake in a 300° oven for 20 minutes. Stir once and bake for 20 minutes more. Sprinkle with Parmesan cheese and toss gently to coat cereal.
    Cool mixture, stirring occasionally. Store in an airtight container in a cool, dry place. Makes 12 (½-cup) servings.

Blazing Trail Mix

  1 6-ounce package mixed
     dried fruit bits
¾ cup broken walnuts
½ cup coconut
½ cup sunflower nuts

● In a mixing bowl combine fruit, walnuts, coconut, and sunflower nuts. Store in an airtight container in a cool, dry place. Makes 11 (¼-cup) servings.

When you're planning to bike or hike, here's a quick pick-up-'n'-go mix.

Pineapple Granola Crunch

¼ cup butter *or* margarine
3 tablespoons sugar
3 tablespoons pineapple
 preserves
1 cup regular rolled oats
½ cup coarsely chopped
 almonds
¼ cup coconut

● In a medium saucepan combine butter or margarine, sugar, and pineapple preserves. Cook over low heat, stirring constantly, till butter is melted and sugar is dissolved. Remove from heat. Stir in oats, almonds, and coconut.

● Spread mixture in an ungreased 13x9x2-inch baking pan. Bake in a 325° oven about 30 minutes or till lightly brown, stirring every 10 minutes.
 Turn mixture onto a large piece of foil. Cool completely. Store in an airtight container in a cool, dry place. Makes 10 (⅓-cup) servings.

Not in the mood for pineapple? Take your pick of apricot, strawberry, or cherry preserves.

Nuts and Stuff

3 cups mixed nuts *or*
 peanuts
2 cups cheese-flavored fish-
 shape crackers
1 cup bite-size corn squares
 cereal
1 cup bite-size wheat
 squares cereal

● In an ungreased 15½x10½x2-inch baking pan combine nuts, crackers, and cereal. Set aside.

Bag up this mix for treats at the kids' Halloween or birthday parties.

⅓ cup butter *or* margarine
1 tablespoon Worcester-
 shire sauce

● In a small saucepan melt butter or margarine. Add Worcestershire sauce. Drizzle over cereal mixture and toss gently to coat cereal evenly.
 Bake in a 300° oven about 40 minutes, stirring every 15 minutes.
 Cool cereal mixture in the pan, stirring occasionally. Store mixture in an airtight container in a cool, dry place. Makes 14 (½-cup) servings.

Five-Spice Walnuts

3 tablespoons butter *or* margarine 1 teaspoon five-spice powder ½ teaspoon salt 3 cups broken walnuts	● In a medium saucepan melt butter or margarine. Stir in five-spice powder and salt. Add broken walnuts, stirring till nuts are evenly coated.	Although you can find five-spice powder in the Oriental section of your grocery store, check your spice rack first. If you have all the spices on hand you can make your own and save yourself a trip to the store. Here's how:
	● Transfer nut mixture to a 13x9x2-inch baking pan. Bake in a 300° oven for 20 minutes, stirring once or twice. Cool in pan for 15 minutes. Turn out onto paper towels to finish cooling. Store tightly covered. Makes 3 cups.	Combine 1 teaspoon *ground cinnamon;* 1 teaspoon crushed *aniseed* or 1 *star anise,* ground; ¼ teaspoon crushed *fennel seed;* ¼ teaspoon freshly ground *pepper* or ¼ teaspoon *Szechuan pepper;* and ⅛ teaspoon *ground cloves.* Store in an airtight container. Makes about 1 tablespoon.

Glazed Pecans

Butter *or* margarine	● Line a baking sheet with foil. Butter the foil, then set baking sheet aside.	Close your eyes as you bite into these sugar-coated pecans and imagine you're eating pecan pie.
2 cups pecan halves, walnut halves, *or* cashews ½ cup sugar 2 tablespoons butter *or* margarine	● In a heavy 10-inch skillet combine nuts, sugar, and butter or margarine. Cook and stir over medium heat for 8 to 9 minutes or till sugar melts and turns a rich brown color.	
½ teaspoon vanilla	● Remove skillet from heat. Immediately stir in vanilla. Spread nut mixture onto the prepared baking sheet. Cool. Break up mixture into clusters. Store tightly covered. Makes 2 cups.	

Caramel Cereal Mix

3 cups bite-size shredded wheat biscuits 3 cups round toasted oat cereal 2 cups pretzel sticks, broken 1½ cups salted peanuts	● Combine shredded wheat biscuits, toasted oat cereal, pretzels, and peanuts in a large buttered roasting pan.
1⅓ cups sugar ¾ cup butter *or* margarine ½ cup light corn syrup 1 teaspoon vanilla	● Butter the sides of 2-quart saucepan. In the pan combine sugar, butter or margarine, and corn syrup. Cook over medium heat to boiling, stirring constantly with a wooden spoon to dissolve sugar. Cook, stirring frequently, till thermometer registers 280°, soft-crack stage. This should take about 10 minutes. Remove saucepan from heat and stir in vanilla.
	● Immediately pour syrup mixture over cereal mixture. Stir gently to coat cereal. Bake in a 350° oven about 20 minutes or till golden brown, stirring once.
	● Transfer cereal mixture onto a large piece of foil. Cool. Break up cereal mixture into small clusters. Store tightly covered. Makes 12 cups.

Fill a box or can full of this buttery crunchy mix when you need a special gift and wrap it in brightly colored paper and ribbon. Whoever is lucky enough to get your package will have as much fun eating the mix as you did making it. And don't forget to tuck in a copy of the recipe—it's sure to be in demand.

Nacho Popcorn

1 teaspoon paprika ½ teaspoon crushed red pepper ½ teaspoon ground cumin ¼ cup butter *or* margarine, melted 10 cups warm popped popcorn ⅓ cup grated Parmesan cheese	● In a small bowl stir paprika, red pepper, and cumin into melted butter or margarine. Gently toss butter mixture with popcorn, coating evenly. Sprinkle with Parmesan cheese and toss till coated. Makes 10 cups.

The next time the between-meal munchies hit you, fight back with this spicy popcorn treat.

Beer and Edam Spread

2 7-ounce rounds Edam cheese	● Bring cheese to room temperature. Cut a circle from the top of each cheese round, about ½ inch from edge. Remove the cut circle of paraffin coating. Carefully scoop cheese out, leaving ½ inch of cheese intact to form a shell. Set shells aside.
1 8-ounce carton dairy sour cream ¼ cup beer 2 teaspoons snipped chives	● Place sour cream, beer, chives, and cheese in a blender container or food processor bowl. Cover and process till smooth, stopping machine occasionally to scrape down sides.
Snipped chives (optional) Assorted crackers	● Spoon cheese mixture into shells. Cover and chill several hours or overnight. (Cover and chill any remaining cheese mixture and use it to refill shells.) Garnish with chives, if desired. Serve with crackers. Makes 3 cups.

Use a spoon to carefully scoop the cheese out, leaving a ½-inch shell. Break the cheese up into fairly small pieces as you put it into the blender or food processor.

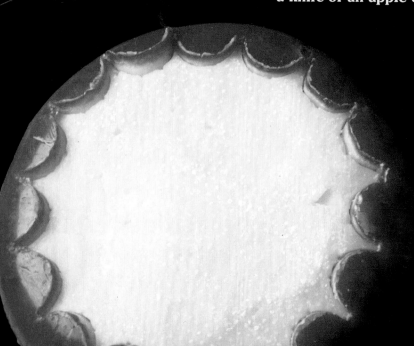

Use a sharp knife to cut a circle through the waxy shell. Cut the scalloped design that's shown with a knife or an apple corer.

Transfer the cheese mixture from the blender or food processor to the cheese shells. Cover filled shells (and any extra spread) with clear plastic wrap and chill till serving time.

Avocado-Chicken Dip

1 cup finely chopped
  cooked chicken *or*
  one 6¾-ounce can
  chunk-style chicken,
  drained and finely
  chopped
1 ripe medium avocado,
  seeded, peeled, and
  chopped
1 small tomato, seeded
  and chopped
¼ cup chopped onion
2 tablespoons rinsed,
  seeded, and chopped
  pickled jalapeño
  peppers
1 clove garlic, minced

● In a mixing bowl stir together the finely chopped cooked chicken or drained and finely chopped canned chicken, chopped avocado, seeded and chopped tomato, chopped onion, seeded and chopped pickled jalapeño peppers, and minced garlic.

This dip has all the ingredients of guacamole, and more. Sour cream gives it a creamy quality and chunks of chicken make it a dip you can sink your teeth into. After a few bites, you'll notice the heat from the jalapeños. You'll come to the conclusion that it's really not like guacamole at all. It's a notch above.

½ cup dairy sour cream
¼ cup milk
2 tablespoons mayonnaise
  or salad dressing
2 teaspoons lemon juice
¼ teaspoon dried oregano,
  crushed
⅛ teaspoon salt

● Stir in the sour cream, milk, mayonnaise or salad dressing, lemon juice, dried oregano, and salt. Stir till ingredients are thoroughly combined. Cover and chill till serving time.

Avocado slices (optional)
Oven-Crisp Tortilla Chips
(see tip box, below) *or*
tortilla chips

● If desired, garnish the dip with avocado slices. Serve with Oven-Crisp Tortilla Chips or other tortilla chips. Makes about 2¾ cups dip.

Oven-Crisp Tortilla Chips

Here's an easy way to make your own tortilla chips without frying them. Cut flour tortillas into wedges with kitchen shears or a knife. Place the wedges on an ungreased baking sheet and toast in a 350° oven for 10 to 12 minutes or till dry and crisp. You'll find they're sturdy for dipping, there's no messy cleanup, and the chips are lower in calories than those you buy in the store.

Meat and Melon Bites

Pictured on the cover.

1 **large honeydew melon**	● Cut melons in half and remove seeds. (*Or,* to prepare scalloped fruit bowl as in photo, see text at right.) Use a melon baller to scoop out pulp. Cut ham or turkey into 1-inch-wide strips.	A fancy melon shell makes a great serving bowl. To make one, first, cut a thin slice off the bottom of a melon so it sits flat. Then, insert a knife at a 45-degree angle into the melon slightly above the middle and cut around the melon in a sawtooth manner.
1 **large cantaloupe**		
1 **3-ounce package very thinly sliced ham** *or* **turkey**		
	● Wrap 1 strip of ham around *each* melon ball, then fasten with a toothpick.	
Lettuce leaves	● Line 1 melon shell with lettuce leaves, then fill with wrapped melon balls. Makes about 60.	

Seafood Cheese Round

2 8-ounce packages cream
   cheese, softened
¼ cup mayonnaise *or* salad
   dressing
2 tablespoons lemon juice
1 teaspoon Worcestershire
   sauce
   Dash garlic powder
½ cup finely chopped celery
1 tablespoon snipped chives
   (optional)

● In a mixer bowl beat cream cheese, mayonnaise or salad dressing, lemon juice, Worcestershire sauce, and garlic powder with an electric mixer till smooth. Stir in celery and chives, if desired.

Keep this quick and easy recipe in mind for potlucks and parties—it makes a great portable appetizer.

¾ cup chili sauce
2 tablespoons sweet pickle
   relish
1 4½-ounce can small
   shrimp, rinsed and
   drained
1 6-ounce can crab meat,
   drained, flaked, and
   cartilage removed
2 tablespoons snipped
   parsley
   Assorted crackers

● Spread cream cheese mixture into a 9-inch pie plate. Combine chili sauce and pickle relish, then spread it over the cream cheese mixture. Sprinkle shrimp and crab meat over chili sauce mixture. Sprinkle parsley over all. Cover and chill several hours. Serve with crackers. Makes 10 to 12 servings.

Broccoli Dip

2 10-ounce packages frozen
   cut broccoli in cheese
   sauce
⅔ cup dairy sour cream
2 tablespoons lemon juice
2 teaspoons minced dried
   onion

● Prepare broccoli in cheese sauce according to package directions. Place cooked broccoli mixture in a blender container or food processor bowl. Add sour cream, lemon juice, and onion. Cover and process till smooth, stopping machine occasionally to scrape down sides. Transfer dip to a serving bowl. Cover and chill for several hours or overnight.

Want extra flavor? Stir 1 teaspoon dried *thyme*, crushed, into the pureed mixture before chilling.

Milk
Assorted vegetable
   dippers
Breadsticks

● Before serving, stir a little bit of milk into dip, if necessary, to make of dipping consistency. Serve with vegetable dippers and breadsticks. Makes 3 cups.

Green Goddess Dip

½ cup dairy sour cream
½ cup mayonnaise *or* salad dressing
½ cup lightly packed parsley *or* watercress
1 tablespoon anchovy paste
2 teaspoons lemon juice
1 teaspoon dried tarragon, crushed
1 green onion, cut up
1 clove garlic, minced
  Assorted vegetable dippers

● In a blender container or food processor bowl combine sour cream, mayonnaise or salad dressing, parsley or watercress, anchovy paste, lemon juice, dried tarragon, green onion, and garlic. Cover and process till smooth. Cover and chill for several hours or overnight. Serve with assorted vegetable dippers. Makes 1⅓ cups.

The ingredients of the classic, creamy-rich salad dressing are transformed into a delicious dip for raw vegetables—especially fresh mushrooms and cherry tomatoes.

Blue Cheese and Brandy Cheese Ball

2 cups shredded cheddar cheese (8 ounces)
1 8-ounce package cream cheese
½ cup crumbled blue cheese
3 tablespoons brandy
2 tablespoons finely chopped onion
1 tablespoon Worcester- shire sauce
  Dash bottled hot pepper sauce
  Dash garlic powder

● Bring cheddar cheese, cream cheese, and blue cheese to room temperature. In a mixer bowl beat cheeses, brandy, onion, Worcestershire sauce, hot pepper sauce, and garlic powder together with an electric mixer till combined. Cover and chill for several hours or overnight.

cheddar cheese

cream cheese

blue cheese

+ brandy

= 1 sensational cheese ball!

¼ cup snipped parsley
¼ cup finely chopped toasted almonds
  Assorted crackers

● Before serving, shape cheese mixture into a ball. Combine parsley and almonds. Roll cheese ball in the parsley-almond mixture. Serve with crackers. Makes 1 ball (about 2⅔ cups).

Video Vittles

Tune in to easy entertaining when you throw a video party.

Whether you invite friends over to enjoy a rented old-west movie on the VCR or ham it up in front of the video camera, you'll want to supply the gang with snacks to munch on during the screening. When your guests arrive, keep these vittles handy for snacking on all evening long. Turn to pages 18 and 19 for the recipes.

MENU
Herb-Buttered
    Pocket Wedges
Three-Layer Spread
Zesty Franks

Zesty Franks

Pictured on pages 16–17.

¼ cup beer
2 teaspoons cornstarch
1½ cups bottled hickory smoke-flavored barbecue sauce
1 10-ounce jar apple jelly
Several dashes bottled hot pepper sauce

● For sauce, in a small saucepan combine beer and cornstarch, then stir in barbecue sauce, apple jelly, and hot pepper sauce. Cook and stir till thickened and bubbly, then cook and stir for 2 minutes more.

1 16-ounce package frankfurters (8 to 10) *or* 1 pound cocktail weiners
1½ cups frozen small whole onions

● Bias-slice franks into bite-size pieces. Stir franks or cocktail weiners and frozen onions into sauce. Cook till heated through. Serve warm. Makes 6 servings.

MENU COUNTDOWN
1 Day Ahead:
Prepare Three-Layer Spread and refrigerate.
Several Hours Ahead:
Prepare Herb-Buttered Pocket Wedges.
15 Minutes Ahead:
Prepare Zesty Franks and keep warm.
During Party:
Serve Zesty Franks in a microwave-safe dish and reheat in a microwave oven when necessary. *Or,* keep them warm by serving in a fondue pot or chafing dish.

Herb-Buttered Pocket Wedges

Pictured on pages 16–17.

2 large pita bread rounds *or* four 7-inch flour tortillas

● Cut each pita round or tortilla into 6 wedges. Gently tear or cut pita wedges in half crosswise to make single layers.

3 tablespoons butter *or* margarine, melted
¼ teaspoon Dijon-style mustard
2 tablespoons snipped parsley
½ teaspoon dried basil, crushed
Dash garlic powder *or* onion powder

● In a small bowl combine melted butter or margarine and mustard. Brush one side of pita or tortilla wedges with butter-mustard mixture. Arrange wedges in a single layer on a baking sheet. In a small bowl combine parsley, basil, and garlic or onion powder. Sprinkle over the wedges. Bake in a 350° oven for 10 to 15 minutes or till crisp and golden brown. Serve warm or cold. Makes 6 servings.

● **Parmesan Pocket Wedges:**
Prepare *Herb-Buttered Pocket Wedges* as directed above, *except* substitute ¼ cup grated *Parmesan or Romano cheese* for the parsley mixture.

For a flavor switch, next time around make these crisp and crunchy snacks using whole wheat pita bread.

Three-Layer Spread

Pictured on pages 16–17.

1 envelope unflavored gelatin ⅓ cup water	● Line a 1-quart mold with plastic wrap, then set aside. In a small saucepan soften unflavored gelatin in water for 5 minutes. Cook and stir over medium heat till gelatin dissolves.
1 8-ounce carton dairy sour cream	● For first layer, stir together sour cream and *2 tablespoons* of the gelatin mixture. Spread evenly in the bottom of the prepared mold. Chill about 20 minutes or till almost firm.
2 medium avocados, peeled, seeded, and mashed 2 tablespoons mayonnaise *or* salad dressing 2 tablespoons lemon juice ¼ teaspoon salt Dash bottled hot pepper sauce	● Meanwhile, for second layer combine avocados, mayonnaise or salad dressing, lemon juice, salt, hot pepper sauce, and *2 tablespoons* of the gelatin mixture. Spread avocado mixture evenly over the sour cream layer. Chill about 20 minutes or till almost set.
6 hard-cooked eggs, finely chopped ¼ cup mayonnaise *or* salad dressing 2 tablespoons snipped parsley 1 tablespoon chopped green onion ¼ teaspoon salt	● For third layer, combine hard-cooked eggs, mayonnaise or salad dressing, parsley, green onion, salt, and remaining gelatin mixture. Spread evenly over avocado layer. Cover and chill overnight.
1 tablespoon chopped pimiento 1 tablespoon bias-sliced green onion Assorted crackers	● Before serving, invert spread onto a serving platter. Remove mold and carefully peel off plastic wrap. Sprinkle chopped pimiento and sliced green onion over the top. Serve with crackers. Makes 6 to 10 servings.

Mold this party spread in a 1-quart bowl if nothing else is available. Line the bowl with plastic wrap and the spread will release easily.

Personality Pizzas

2 packages (10 each)
  refrigerated biscuits
1 15½-ounce jar pizza sauce
  Ground Beef and
    Mushroom Topper
  Pepperoni Topper
  Mexicali Topper

● Separate biscuits, then cut each one in half. Roll each half into a ball. Flatten balls into 2- to 2½-inch circles on an ungreased baking sheet. Spread about *1 heaping teaspoon* pizza sauce over *each* biscuit, spreading to within ¼ inch of edge. Add desired topper. Bake in a 425° oven for 10 to 12 minutes or till golden brown. Serve warm. Makes 40.

● **Ground Beef and Mushroom Topper:** Cook ½ pound *ground beef* and ½ cup chopped *onion* till meat is browned. Drain off fat. Drain two 4-ounce cans *sliced mushrooms,* and stir into ground beef. Top flattened biscuits with beef mixture and 1 cup shredded *mozzarella cheese.*

● **Pepperoni Topper:** Place 1 thin slice *pepperoni* on each flattened biscuit. Top biscuits with 1 cup sliced *green pepper* and 1 cup shredded *cheddar cheese.*

● **Mexicali Topper:** Top flattened biscuits with one 4½-ounce can *sliced pitted ripe olives* (about ½ cup) and 1 cup shredded *mozzarella or hot pepper cheese.*

Don't be caught offguard when unexpected guests ring your doorbell. Bake a bunch of these miniature pizzas, store them in your freezer, and surprise your guests with a quick snack. Pop as many individual pizzas as needed into a 350° oven for 9 to 10 minutes.

Sausage-Stuffed Mushrooms

18 fresh large mushrooms (about 1 pound)	● Wash mushrooms gently in cold water; pat dry. Remove stems, reserving caps. Finely chop the stems; set aside.
2 tablespoons butter *or* margarine **1 tablespoon dry sherry**	● In a 10-inch skillet melt butter or margarine. Add 1 tablespoon dry sherry and the mushroom caps; cook on medium heat for 2 to 3 minutes or till mushrooms caps are slightly golden. Remove with a slotted spoon; drain on paper towels.
¼ pound bulk Italian sausage **2 tablespoons finely chopped onion** **1 clove garlic, minced**	● Add sausage, onion, and garlic to the skillet. Cook about 5 minutes or till sausage is brown and onion is tender. Add the reserved stems and cook 2 minutes more. Remove from heat; drain.
¼ cup fine dry bread crumbs **¼ cup grated Parmesan cheese** **1 tablespoon dry sherry** **Sliced pimiento**	● Mix in bread crumbs, *2 tablespoons* of the Parmesan cheese, and 1 tablespoon dry sherry. Place a rounded tablespoon of the sausage mixture in each cap. Arrange the stuffed mushroom caps in a 12x7½x2-inch baking dish. Bake in a 350° oven for 10 to 15 minutes or till hot. Sprinkle with the remaining Parmesan cheese. Garnish with sliced pimiento. Makes 18.

Italian sausage spices up the stuffing for these mushrooms. Keep in mind that Italian sausage can vary in seasoning depending on the brand you buy. The spicier the sausage, the spicier these appetizers will be.

Beef Bundles with Red Mustard Dip

½ pound lean ground beef
2 tablespoons sliced green onion
1 single-serving envelope *instant* tomato soup mix
¼ cup chopped water chestnuts
¼ teaspoon black pepper
⅛ teaspoon ground ginger

● In a skillet cook ground beef and sliced green onion till meat is brown and onion is tender; drain well. Stir in one envelope instant tomato soup mix, chopped water chestnuts, black pepper, ground ginger, and ¼ cup *water* till well combined.

1 17¼-ounce package (2 sheets) frozen puff pastry, thawed according to package directions

● Cut each pastry sheet into nine 3-inch squares. Put a rounded tablespoon of filling on each. Fold into triangles. Seal edges with fork. Place on a baking sheet. Cover; chill for 3 to 24 hours.

½ cup hot water
1 single-serving envelope *instant* tomato soup mix
2 tablespoons dry mustard
2 teaspoons paprika
1 tablespoon vinegar

● Bake pastries in a 400° oven about 15 minutes or till golden.
For dip, combine hot water and one envelope instant tomato soup mix; cool. Combine with dry mustard and paprika; let stand 10 minutes. Stir in vinegar. If desired, garnish with tomato rose and parsley. Serve with pastries. Makes 18.

French, Chinese, and American cuisines are represented in these classy hors d'oeuvres. The French take credit for the puff pastry, the Chinese contribute the pungent mustard dip, and the Americans make them easier with the use of convenience products.

Super Nachos

4 cups tortilla chips ½ pound bulk Italian sausage, chorizo, *or* ground beef	● Spread tortilla chips about one layer deep (overlapping slightly) on an 11- or 12-inch ovenproof platter. Set platter aside. In a skillet cook Italian sausage, chorizo, or ground beef till browned, then drain off fat. Pat with paper towels to remove additional fat.
1½ cups shredded cheddar, American, *or* mozzarella cheese (6 ounces)	● Sprinkle meat evenly over tortilla chips. Sprinkle cheese over meat. Bake in a 350° oven for 5 to 7 minutes or till cheese melts.
1 8-ounce container frozen avocado dip, thawed ½ cup dairy sour cream Sliced ripe olives Sliced jalapeño peppers Sliced pickled cherry peppers	● To serve, spoon avocado dip over meat and cheese, then top with sour cream. Sprinkle with olives, jalapeño peppers, and cherry peppers. Serves 8.
	● **Cheese Nachos:** Spread tortilla chips on a platter as directed above. Sprinkle with 1 cup shredded *Monterey Jack cheese* and ½ cup shredded *cheddar* or *American cheese*. Bake as directed above. Sprinkle with 2 tablespoons canned *green chili peppers*, seeded and chopped, if desired.

Throw together a tossed salad, build a plateful of these nifty nachos, and you've made an easy supper for four!

Making Wontons

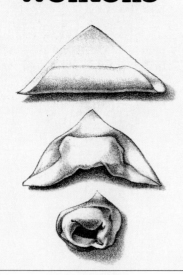

Mastered the egg rolls at right? Use the skins and filling for another Chinese specialty—wontons!

Cut each of the 12 egg roll skins into quarters, making a total of 48 (3½-inch) squares. Position a square with one point toward you. Spoon a scant *1 tablespoon* of the filling just below the center of the square. Fold the bottom point of the square over the filling, tucking the point under the filling.

Roll once toward the center, covering the filling and leaving about 1 inch unrolled at the top of the square. Moisten the right corner of the square with water. Grasp corners and bring them toward you, below the filling, till they meet. Lap the right corner over the left corner, then press to seal securely. Fry wontons in deep hot oil as directed in egg roll recipe.

Egg Rolls

12 egg roll skins Chicken-Curry Filling	● Place egg roll skin with one point toward you. Spoon about ¼ cup filling diagonally across and just below center of egg roll skin. Fold bottom point of skin over filling, tucking the point under the filling.	**Half the fun of eating egg rolls and wontons is plunging them into zesty sauces—ones that offer contrasting flavors. For example, match Sweet and Sour Sauce (see recipe, below) with Dijon-style mustard.**
	● Fold side corners over, forming an envelope shape. Roll up egg roll toward remaining corner, then moisten point and press firmly to seal. Repeat with the remaining egg roll skins and filling.	
Cooking oil for deep-fat frying	● In a heavy saucepan, fry egg rolls, a few at a time, in deep hot oil (365°) for 2 to 3 minutes or till golden brown. Drain on paper towels. Serve warm with one or two sauces (see tip, right). Makes 12 egg rolls.	

Chicken-Curry Filling

2 cups chopped cabbage 2 tablespoons chopped green onion 1 clove garlic, minced 1 tablespoon cooking oil 2 cups finely chopped cooked chicken	● In a skillet cook cabbage, green onion, and garlic in hot oil for 2 to 3 minutes or till cabbage is crisp-tender. Remove from heat and stir in chicken.	**Sweet and Sour Sauce: In a small saucepan combine ½ cup *packed brown sugar* and 1 tablespoon *cornstarch*. Stir in ⅓ cup *chicken broth*, ⅓ cup *red wine vinegar*, 1 table-spoon *soy sauce*, ½ teaspoon *grated gingerroot*, and 2 *cloves garlic*, minced. Cook and stir till thickened and bubbly, then cook and stir for 2 minutes more. Serve warm or cold with Egg Rolls. Makes about 1 cup.**
1 beaten egg 2 tablespoons dry red wine *or* water 1 teaspoon curry powder ¼ teaspoon salt	● In a small bowl combine egg, wine or water, curry powder, and salt, then stir into chicken mixture. Use to make Egg Rolls (see recipe, above). Makes 3 cups.	

Home-Run Hits

½ cup refried beans
  Dash garlic powder
2 cups chopped frankfurters
  (about 6)
1 cup shredded cheddar
  cheese (4 ounces)

● In a large bowl stir together the refried beans and garlic powder. Stir in chopped franks and cheddar cheese.

Right off the bat, kids' noses know whether or not something smells good. You'll never strike out with these aromatic frank- and bean-filled baseball look-alikes.

2 8-ounce packages
  refrigerated crescent
  rolls
  Barbecue sauce *or* catsup

● For *each* ball, flatten *2* roll triangles to form a rectangle, pinching perforations together to seal. Press into muffin cups. Place about ⅓ *cup* of the meat mixture in the center. One at a time, fold *3* corners of dough over the filling. Fold the remaining corner of dough completely over the top, stretching to fit. Seal.

　Bake in a 375° oven for 18 to 20 minutes or till golden. Cover loosely with foil during last few minutes, if necessary, to prevent overbrowning. Transfer to a wire rack. Serve warm with barbecue sauce or catsup. Makes 8.

Cocktail Party for 12 or 24

Cocktail parties are always "in" because they're a simple and informal way to entertain lots of people without a lot of work. Whether you're welcoming new neighbors to the block, celebrating a promotion, or just enjoying an evening with friends, you'll find making this menu is fun (see recipes, pages 30–33). What's more, you'll be amazed how easily the foods go together—whether your gathering is for 12 or 24.

MENU
Barbecued Mini Drums
Smoky Cheese Log
Avocado Dip
Sangria Sipper

MENU COUNTDOWN
1 Week Ahead:
Prepare Smoky Cheese Log and freeze.
1 Day Ahead:
Remove Smoky Cheese Log from freezer and thaw in refrigerator.
4 Hours Ahead:
Combine wine and iced tea mix for Sangria Sipper. Add orange and lemon slices and refrigerate. Prepare Avocado Dip and vegetable dippers and refrigerate.

1½ Hours Ahead:
Prepare Barbecued Mini Drums.
Just Before Party:
Stir carbonated water into Sangria Sipper. Garnish with lemon slices, wedges, or both.

Barbecued Chicken Wings

Pictured on pages 28–29.

For 12

For 24

For 12		For 24
12 chicken wings (about 2 pounds)	● Cut off and discard tips of chicken wings. Cut wings at joints to form 24 (or 48) pieces. Place the 24 chicken wing pieces in a single layer in an ungreased 13x9x2-inch baking pan. (Use a 15x10x1-inch shallow baking pan for 48 pieces.) Bake in a 375° oven for 20 minutes. Drain well.	**24 chicken wings (about 4 pounds)**
¼ **cup catsup** 2 **tablespoons water** 2 **tablespoons finely chopped onion** 1 **tablespoon cooking oil** 1½ **teaspoons vinegar** 1 **teaspoon brown sugar** 1 **teaspoon Worcestershire sauce** ¼ **teaspoon dried oregano, crushed** ¼ **teaspoon chili powder** ¼ **teaspoon dry mustard** 1 **bay leaf** 1 **clove garlic, minced**	● Meanwhile, for barbecue sauce, in a saucepan combine catsup, water, onion, cooking oil, vinegar, brown sugar, Worcestershire sauce, oregano, chili powder, mustard, bay leaf, and garlic. Bring mixture to boiling, then reduce heat. Simmer, covered, for 10 minutes, stirring occasionally. Discard bay leaf.	½ **cup catsup** ¼ **cup water** ¼ **cup finely chopped onion** 2 **tablespoons cooking oil** 1 **tablespoon vinegar** 2 **teaspoons brown sugar** 2 **teaspoons Worcestershire sauce** ½ **teaspoon dried oregano, crushed** ½ **teaspoon chili powder** ½ **teaspoon dry mustard** 2 **bay leaves** 2 **cloves garlic, minced**
	● Brush barbecue sauce on the partially baked chicken wings. Bake for 10 minutes, then turn and brush barbecue sauce on the other side. Bake for 5 to 10 minutes more or till chicken is tender. Makes 12 or 24 servings.	

Smoky Cheese Log

Pictured on pages 28–29.

For 12

For 24

For 12		For 24
½ of an 8-ounce package cream cheese, cut up (4 ounces)	● Bring cream cheese, cheddar cheese, Swiss cheese, and butter or margarine to room temperature. In a mixer bowl beat cheeses and butter or margarine with an electric mixer till combined. Beat in wine or milk and horseradish. Cover and chill for 2 hours.	1 8-ounce package cream cheese, cut up
¾ cup shredded smoked cheddar cheese (3 ounces)		1½ cups shredded smoked cheddar cheese (6 ounces)
¼ cup shredded Swiss cheese (1 ounce)		½ cup shredded Swiss cheese (2 ounces)
2 tablespoons butter *or* margarine, cut up		¼ cup butter *or* margarine, cut up
1 tablespoon dry white wine *or* milk		2 tablespoons dry white wine *or* milk
½ teaspoon prepared horseradish		1 teaspoon prepared horseradish
¼ cup finely chopped pecans *or* walnuts	● Combine pecans or walnuts and parsley. On waxed paper shape cheese mixture into a log about 6 inches long (when serving 24, shape into 2 logs). Roll log in nut-parsley mixture, pressing lightly into log. Wrap in clear plastic wrap. Chill about 3 hours or till firm. To serve, unwrap and serve with crackers. Makes 1 or 2 logs.	½ cup finely chopped pecans *or* walnuts
2 tablespoons snipped parsley		¼ cup snipped parsley
Assorted crackers		Assorted crackers

Tomato-Avocado Dip

Pictured on pages 28–29.

For 12		For 24
2 slices bacon	● In a small skillet cook bacon till crisp. Drain well. Crumble bacon and set aside.	4 slices bacon
1 large avocado, halved, seeded, and peeled 1 medium tomato, peeled, seeded, and finely chopped ½ cup dairy sour cream ¼ cup grated Parmesan cheese 2 green onions, finely chopped 1 tablespoon lemon juice Dash bottled hot pepper sauce 1 tablespoon milk (optional)	● In a medium bowl mash avocado. Stir in tomato, sour cream, Parmesan cheese, green onion, lemon juice, hot pepper sauce, and reserved bacon. Add milk to thin the consistency of the dip, if desired.	2 large avocados, halved, seeded, and peeled 2 medium tomatoes, peeled, seeded, and finely chopped 1 cup dairy sour cream ½ cup grated Parmesan cheese 4 green onions, finely chopped 2 tablespoons lemon juice Several dashes bottled hot pepper sauce 2 tablespoons milk (optional)
Assorted vegetable dippers	● Transfer mixture to a serving bowl. Cover and chill. Serve with vegetable dippers. Makes 2 or 4 cups.	Assorted vegetable dippers

Sangria Sipper

Pictured on pages 28–29.

For 12

- 2 750-milliliter bottles rosé wine, chilled
- ¾ cup sugar-and-lemon-flavored iced tea mix
- 1 orange, thinly sliced
- 1 lemon, thinly sliced (optional)
- 2 10-ounce bottles carbonated water, chilled
- 1 cup sliced fresh strawberries (optional)
- Ice

● In a large pitcher combine rosé wine and iced tea mix. Add orange slices and lemon slices, if desired. Cover and chill. Just before serving, pour carbonated water down the side of the pitcher. Gently stir in sliced fresh strawberries, if desired. Serve over ice. Makes 12 or 24 (8-ounce) servings.

For 24

- 4 750-milliliter bottles rosé wine, chilled
- 1½ cups sugar-and-lemon-flavored iced tea mix
- 2 oranges, thinly sliced
- 1 lemon, thinly sliced (optional)
- 4 10-ounce bottles carbonated water, chilled
- 2 cups sliced fresh strawberries (optional)
- Ice

What Should I Serve?

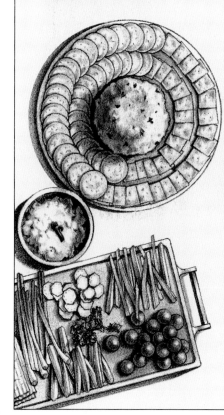

Deciding what foods to serve at a party is always a tough decision—there are so many delicious choices. Here are some tips to keep in mind when planning your menu.

● Serve a combination of hot and cold appetizers. How many of each depends on your refrigerator space and how many appetizers you can keep warm at once.

● Team-up foods with contrasting textures—crisp and crunchy crackers and vegetables work well with creamy dips or spreads.

● Consider flavors and foods that will appeal to your guests. If you don't know what they like, stick to mildly flavored foods. For adventuresome friends, pick out some exotic recipes you've been dying to try.

● Choose appetizers with a variety of flavors. For example, foods all flavored with curry or chili powder will end up tasting the same.

● If you're also serving a meal, match your appetizers to the theme of the meal—Italian antipasto with spaghetti or Chinese egg rolls with moo shu pork.

● Remember that *you* are a part of your party. Avoid dishes that keep you in the kitchen, away from your guests and the fun!

Peanut-Butter-Chip Muffins

1½ cups all-purpose flour
⅓ cup sugar
2½ teaspoons baking powder
¼ teaspoon salt
½ cup chunk-style
      peanut butter
 2 tablespoons butter *or*
      margarine
 2 beaten eggs
¾ cup milk
½ of a 6-ounce package
      (½ cup) semisweet
      chocolate pieces

● In a medium bowl stir together the flour, sugar, baking powder, and salt. With a pastry blender or 2 knives, cut in the peanut butter and the butter till the mixture resembles coarse crumbs.

In a bowl combine the eggs and milk. Add all at once to flour mixture. Stir just till moistened. Batter should be lumpy. Fold in chocolate pieces.

Muffins make great additions to picnics and satisfying snacking for camping trips or long car trips. Make a batch and freeze some for quick take-alongs later.

● Grease muffin cups or line with paper bake cups. Fill ⅔ full, as shown below. Bake in a 400° oven for 15 to 17 minutes or till lightly golden. Remove from muffin cups. Cool. Makes 12.

After you've baked the muffins, remove them from the pans and cool. Then pack the muffins in an airtight containter and store them at room temperature for several days or in the freezer up to four months.

Fill the greased or paper-bake-cup-lined muffin cups just two-thirds full. If you fill them full, the batter will run over as the muffins bake.

Pocket Pies

¾ **cup whole wheat flour** ⅓ **cup all-purpose flour** 2 **tablespoons toasted wheat germ** ¼ **teaspoon salt** ⅛ **teaspoon ground cinnamon**	● In a mixing bowl stir together whole wheat flour, all-purpose flour, wheat germ, salt, and cinnamon.
⅓ **cup shortening** 3 **to 4 tablespoons cold milk**	● Cut in shortening till pieces are the size of small peas. Sprinkle *1 tablespoon* of the milk over part of the mixture. Gently toss with a fork. Push to side of bowl. Repeat till all is moistened. On a lightly floured surface roll dough into an 11-inch square. Cut into four 5½-inch squares.
1 **large apple** *or* 2 **medium peaches** *or* **pears**	● Remove and discard core or pit from fruit. Peel and chop fruit. Place ¼ of the fruit on half of *each* square of dough.
2 **tablespoon brown sugar** ¼ **teaspoon ground cinnamon** ⅛ **teaspoon ground nutmeg** 2 **tablespoons butter** *or* **margarine**	● In a small bowl stir together brown sugar, cinnamon, and nutmeg. Sprinkle over fruit. Dot with some of the butter.
Milk **Sugar (optional)**	● Moisten edges of squares with a little milk. Shape into rectangles by folding squares in half over fruit mixture. With the tines of a fork, press edges to seal. Place on an ungreased baking sheet and make small slashes to allow steam to escape. Brush with milk and sprinkle with additional sugar, if desired. Bake in a 375° oven for 14 to 18 minutes or till brown on *edges*. Transfer to a wire rack. Serve warm or cool. Makes 4.

Legend says that once upon a time, a little prince loved the tart and tangy taste of fruit *so* much that he wanted a way to carry it with him everywhere. One night he waited until he saw the first evening star and made a wish. He awoke the next morning to find the magical answer—these easy-to-tote pies.

Try this pizza for dessert! It's easy enough for a quick treat but special enough to make for a birthday party.

Rocky Road Pizza

1 cup butter *or* margarine (2 sticks) ½ cup sugar ½ cup packed brown sugar	● Turn oven to 375°. In a large mixer bowl beat butter or margarine with electric mixer on medium speed till softened (about 30 seconds). Add sugar and brown sugar and beat till fluffy.
1 egg 1 teaspoon vanilla 1¾ cups all-purpose flour	● Add egg and vanilla. Beat well. With mixer on low speed gradually beat in flour. Spread dough evenly in an ungreased 14-inch pizza pan.
1 cup peanuts 1 cup tiny marshmallows 1 6-ounce package (1 cup) semisweet chocolate pieces	● Bake in the 375° oven about 12 minutes or till golden. Sprinkle peanuts, marshmallows, and semisweet chocolate pieces atop hot crust. (If you like, make each section of the pizza different by sprinkling different combinations on each section.)
	● Return pizza to the 375° oven. Bake 6 to 8 minutes more or till marshmallows are golden. Cool in pan on cooling rack.
	● To serve pizza, cut into wedges or squares with a pizza cutter or sharp knife. Makes about 32 pieces.

Spread dough evenly in pizza pan with a metal spatula or knife. Bake.

Scatter peanuts, tiny marshmallows, and chocolate chips over the hot crust and finish baking.

Cut this pizza into wedges or squares, as you would any pizza. To make the pizza pieces easier to eat, first cut 16 wedges. Then cut a circle in the pizza as shown, cutting each wedge in two.

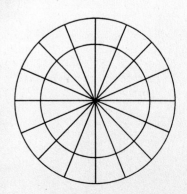

These tasty turtles are a snap to shape. They have pecan feet, candy-stuffed cookie bodies, and chocolate shells.

Shape the dough into 1-inch balls. Press a piece of candy into each ball and mold the dough around it.

For feet, arrange on ungreased cookie sheets groups of 4 pecan halves so their ends touch. Space groups 2 inches apart.

Put a ball of candy-stuffed dough atop each group of pecan halves.

Snapping Turtles

6 tablespoons butter *or* margarine **⅓ cup shortening** **⅔ cup packed brown sugar**	● In a large mixer bowl beat butter or margarine and shortening with electric mixer on medium speed 30 seconds. Add brown sugar and beat till fluffy.
1 egg **1 teaspoon vanilla**	● Add egg and vanilla. Beat well.
1¾ cups all-purpose flour **½ teaspoon baking soda** **½ teaspoon baking powder** **¼ teaspoon salt**	● Stir together flour, baking soda, baking powder, and salt. Gradually add flour mixture to butter mixture, beating well. Cover and chill in the refrigerator about 1 hour or till firm enough to handle.
Pecan halves **Assorted candy***	● Turn oven to 325°. Follow directions above for shaping turtles.
	● Bake in the 325° oven for 15 to 20 minutes. Let cool on cookie sheets 1 minute. With a pancake turner lift cookies onto a cooling rack to finish cooling.
1 6-ounce package (1 cup) semisweet chocolate pieces	● In small saucepan melt chocolate pieces over low heat. Spread atop cookies. Store in refrigerator. Makes 48.

*Note: Candies that work best are ½-inch pieces of chocolate-covered nougat bars with peanuts or caramel, candy-coated milk chocolate-covered peanuts, and chocolate-coated caramel candies.

Adam's Apple Cake

1¼ cups all-purpose flour ½ teaspoon baking soda ½ teaspoon ground cinnamon ¼ teaspoon salt ¼ cup butter *or* margarine	● In a medium mixing bowl combine flour, baking soda, cinnamon, and salt. Cut in butter or margarine till the mixture resembles coarse crumbs.
1 beaten egg ½ cup applesauce ⅓ cup light molasses	● In a small mixing bowl stir together egg, applesauce, and molasses; stir into flour mixture just till moistened.
¼ cup raisins	● Stir in raisins. Turn into a greased and floured 8x8x2-inch baking pan. Bake in a 350° oven for 25 to 30 minutes or till a wooden toothpick inserted in the center comes out clean. Cool in the pan 15 minutes. Remove from pan, if desired.
¾ cup sifted powdered sugar 4 teaspoons lemon juice	● Combine powdered sugar and lemon juice; spread over warm cake. Serve warm or cool. Makes 9 servings.

Applesauce gives this snack cake its moistness and makes it a good keeper. With hungry snackers around, however, you may never find out how well it stores.

Carrot Cupcakes

1 4½-ounce jar strained
     carrots (baby food)
¼ cup packed brown sugar
1 egg
2 tablespoons cooking oil
⅛ teaspoon finely shredded
     orange peel
	● In a small mixing bowl reserve *1 tablespoon* of the strained carrots for frosting; cover and set aside.
	     In a medium mixing bowl combine remaining carrots, brown sugar, egg, oil, and ⅛ teaspoon orange peel; beat with a wire whisk or fork till smooth.

1 cup packaged biscuit mix	● Add biscuit mix; beat just till mixed. Spoon into greased or paper-bake-cup-lined muffin cups, filling two-thirds full. Bake in a 375° oven for 15 to 20 minutes or till a wooden toothpick inserted in center comes out clean. Remove cupcakes. Cool on a wire rack.

1 tablespoon butter *or*
     margarine, softened
⅛ teaspoon finely shredded
     orange peel
½ to ¾ cup sifted powdered
     sugar
	● For frosting, add softened butter or margarine and ⅛ teaspoon orange peel to the reserved carrots. Gradually stir in enough powdered sugar to make of spreading consistency. Frost cupcakes. Makes 6.

No need to shred carrots for these little carrot cakes! Take the easy route and use a jar of baby food instead.

Frosty Cookiewiches

1 17-ounce roll
     refrigerated sugar
     cookie dough
   Sherbet Filling, Pudding
   Filling, *or* Fruit 'n'
   Cheese Filling

● Slice and bake the cookie dough according to package directions.

Use one of the filling variations below to assemble the cookies into sandwiches.

Place cookie sandwiches on a baking sheet, then loosely cover and freeze till firm. If desired, wrap each sandwich in a 6-inch-square piece of foil and continue freezing till serving time. Makes 18.

Sherbet Filling: Spoon 1 quart of softened *orange, lemon, lime,* or *raspberry sherbet* into 3 clean 12-ounce juice cans or 10-ounce soup cans. Cover the open end of each can with foil and freeze till sherbet is firm.

To assemble cookies, remove the foil and other end from the sherbet-filled can. Press on one end, forcing sherbet roll out. With a sharp knife, cut sherbet roll into 6 slices. Place a slice between 2 cookies. Freeze as directed above.

● **Pudding Filling:** In a mixing bowl stir together one 17½-ounce can *chocolate pudding,* ½ cup toasted *coconut,* and ½ cup chopped *pecans.*

To assemble cookies, spread *half* of the cookies with the pudding mixture, using about 2 tablespoons for each. Top each with a second cookie. Freeze as directed above.

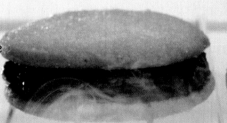

● **Fruit 'n' Cheese Filling:** In a bowl stir together two 8-ounce containers soft-style *cream cheese with pineapple* or *strawberry,* ½ cup drained *crushed pineapple,* and 1 tablespoon *sugar.*

To assemble cookies, spread *half* of the cookies with the mixture, using about 2 tablespoons for each. Top each with a second cookie. Freeze as directed above.

Muchas Margaritas

6 ounces tequila (¾ cup)
4 ounces frozen limeade concentrate (½ cup)
⅓ cup orange liqueur
20 to 24 ice cubes (about 3 cups)

● In a blender container combine tequila, concentrate, and orange liqueur. Cover and blend till smooth. With blender running, add ice cubes, one at a time, through hole in lid, blending till slushy. Pour into prepared glasses (see tip, right). Makes 8 (4-ounce) servings.

● **Very Berry Margaritas:** In a blender container combine the tequila, limeade concentrate, and orange liqueur. Add one 10-ounce package *frozen strawberries,* broken up. Cover and blend until smooth. Add ice as directed for Muchas Margaritas.

● **Gorgeous Grape Margaritas:** In a blender container combine the tequila, one 6-ounce can frozen *grape juice concentrate,* and orange liqueur. Omit limeade concentrate. Cover and blend until smooth. Add ice as directed for Muchas Margaritas.

● **Banana Margaritas:** In a blender container combine the tequila, limeade concentrate, orange liqueur, and 2 cups cut-up ripe *bananas.* Cover and blend until smooth. Add ice as directed for Muchas Margaritas.

● **Apricotta Margaritas:** In a blender container combine the tequila, limeade concentrate, orange liqueur, and one 16-ounce can *unpeeled apricot halves or peach slices,* drained. Cover and blend until smooth. Add ice as directed for Muchas Margaritas.

For lots of folks, a margarita without salt is like a movie without popcorn. Give your margaritas that bartender's flair by rubbing the rim of each glass with a little lime juice or a lime wedge. Invert glasses into a shallow dish of coarse salt, then shake off excess salt.

Frozen Daiquiri Slush

Try a trick similar to the one for margaritas when you're serving daiquiris. Rub the rim of your glasses in water, and dip them into granulated or powdered sugar.

3 cups water
1 6-ounce can frozen lemonade concentrate
1 6-ounce can frozen limeade concentrate
1 juice can rum (¾ cup)
¼ cup sugar

● In a medium mixing bowl stir together water, lemonade concentrate, limeade concentrate, rum, and sugar. Pour into a 9x5x3-inch loaf pan. Cover pan with foil. Freeze overnight.

Lime wedges (optional)

● To serve, scrape the top of the frozen mixture with a spoon to form a slush. Spoon slush into chilled glasses. Garnish with lime wedges, if desired. Makes about 6 (8-ounce) servings.

● **Frozen Fruit Daiquiri Slush:** In a blender container place one 16-ounce package frozen *unsweetened peach slices,* one 10-ounce package frozen *sliced strawberries, or* one 10-ounce package frozen *red raspberries;* add ¾ cup *rum.* Cover and blend till smooth. Transfer to a large mixing bowl. Stir in 3 cups *water,* one 6-ounce can frozen *lemonade concentrate,* and one 6-ounce can frozen *limeade concentrate.* Freeze and serve as directed above. Makes about 8 (8-ounce) servings.

Cranberry-Wine Cocktail

2 cups rosé wine *or* burgundy, chilled
2 cups cranberry juice cocktail, chilled
1 6-ounce can frozen pineapple juice concentrate

● In a large pitcher combine rosé wine or burgundy, cranberry cocktail, and pineapple concentrate, stirring until concentrate is dissolved.

This full-bodied drink easily converts into a winter warm-up. Heat it on the stove or in the microwave, then serve in mugs.

Frozen pineapple chunks, *or* frosted fresh cranberries (optional)

● Pour into chilled cocktail or wineglasses. Garnish each with frozen pineapple chunks or frosted cranberries on a toothpick, if desired. Makes about 10 (4-ounce) servings.

Creamy Coffee Liqueur Punch

½ cup coffee liqueur
¼ cup milk
2 tablespoons crème de cacao
1 quart vanilla ice cream

● In a blender container combine coffee liqueur, milk, and crème de cacao. Spoon in vanilla ice cream. Cover and blend till smooth.

Beautiful chocolate curls are as easy as a flick of the wrist when you follow our directions.

Chocolate curls (optional) (see tip, right)

● Pour mixture into chilled glasses. Garnish with chocolate curls, if desired. Makes about 6 (4-ounce) servings.

 Let a bar of milk chocolate come to room temperature. Carefully draw a vegetable peeler across the chocolate, allowing the chocolate to curl as you pull. (For small curls, use one of the narrow sides of the chocolate; for large curls, use one of the wide surfaces.) Transfer the curls to the drinks by inserting a toothpick through one end and carefully lifting.

Strawberries Through a Straw

3 cups frozen unsweetened strawberries 1½ cups unsweetened pineapple juice 2 tablespoons honey (optional)	● In a blender container combine frozen strawberries, pineapple juice, and honey, if desired. Cover and blend till smooth. Makes 4 (6-ounce) servings.	**Sipping strawberries through a straw is hard to do, unless you spin them in a blender with some fruit juice. If you like, sweeten this 100% natural drink with a little honey.**

Chocolate-Peanut-Banana Swirl

1 medium banana	● Cut the banana into 1-inch pieces. Wrap pieces in foil and freeze.	**It looks like a chocolate milk shake but your taste buds will tell you it's much, much more.** **Freeze the banana before blending the shake to make every sip refreshingly cold.**
1 cup milk 1 cup chocolate ice cream ¼ cup creamy peanut butter	● Unwrap the banana pieces. In a blender container combine banana, milk, chocolate ice cream, and peanut butter. Cover and blend till smooth. Makes 3 (6-ounce) servings.	

Push-Button Peach Cream

1 cup frozen unsweetened peach slices* or one 8¾-ounce can peach slices, chilled and drained ½ of an 8-ounce carton (½ cup) vanilla yogurt ¼ cup milk ⅛ teaspoon ground nutmeg	● In a blender container combine frozen or canned peach slices, vanilla yogurt, milk, and ⅛ teaspoon nutmeg. Cover the blender container; blend till the mixture is smooth.	**With the push of a button on an electric blender, you can turn peaches and yogurt into a thick and creamy shake.**
Ground nutmeg	● Pour into two small glasses. Sprinkle each with a little more nutmeg. Makes 2 (4-ounce) servings. ***Note:** If you use frozen peach slices, add 1 tablespoon *honey* to the mixture before blending.	

Creamy Coolers

½ cup sugar
1 envelope *unsweetened* soft drink mix (any flavor)

● Stir together sugar and fruit-flavored drink mix; store in a tightly covered container till ready to use.

Milk
Vanilla ice cream

● For 1 serving, in a blender container combine *1 cup* of milk, *1 small scoop* of vanilla ice cream, and *1 to 2 tablespoons* of the soft drink mixture. Cover and blend till smooth. Pour into a glass. Makes 1 (12-ounce) serving.

For 4 to 6 servings, in a blender container combine *2 cups* of milk, *4 to 6 small scoops* of vanilla ice cream, and *⅓ to ½ cup* of the soft drink mixture. Cover and blend till smooth. Stir in *2 cups* more milk. Pour into glasses. Makes 4 to 6 (12-ounce) servings.

Wow! Pink lemonade, lemon-lime, grape, orange, black cherry, strawberry, raspberry, lemonade . . . pick your favorite fruit flavor and make a shake.

Index